CREATING THE LIFE OF YOUR DREAMS

A step by step guide to vision boarding

KAREN TUI BOYES

Published by Spectrum Education Limited, P O Box 30 818, Lower Hutt, New Zealand

ISBN 978-0-9951314-0-8 (Paperback)

ISBN 978-0-9951314-1-5 (e-book)

Text copyright © Karen Tui Boyes 2020

Designed and typeset by Spectrum Education, New Zealand

All rights reserved. No part of this publication may be reproduced, stored in a retrieval system, or transmitted in any form or by any means (electronic, mechanical, photocopying or otherwise), without the prior written permission of both the copyright owner and the publisher of this book.

To Tui & Trevor – thanks for encouraging me to follow my passions, even when you didn't totally understand my why. You are great role models to making the most of each day and living your best life. You continue to inspire me by taking the opportunities given, creating and providing joy and happiness to all those you meet and making every day a great day.

To all my readers and followers – may you live the life of your dreams and create a positive impact on the world.

ABOUT THE AUTHOR

Karen Tui Boyes is a champion for Life Long Learning across nations, industries and organisations. She is the author of *Creating An Effective Learning Environment*, *Project Genius, Your Weekly Gratitude Focus Quote Book*, and *Study Smart* and the creator of the Teachers Matter Magazine, Teachers Matter Conferences, Study Smart Boardgame, Study Smart Workshops and the Habits of Mind Bootcamp.

Karen is the CEO of Spectrum Education, Affiliate Director of the Institute for the Habits of Mind, and was awarded NZ Educator of the Year in 2014 & 2017, NZ Speaker of the Year in 2013 & 2019, and NZ Business Woman of the Year in 2001.

A sought after speaker who continually gets rave reviews from audiences around the world, Karen has presented across six continents, in 20 countries, and turns the latest educational research into easy-to-implement strategies and techniques. She is extremely passionate about people developing personally as well as professionally.

She is the wife of one and mother of two.

CONTENTS

About the Author IV

Introduction 1

    1. Getting Started 5

    2. Review – reflecting back 7

    3. Getting Clear 9

    4. Brag List 11

    5. Spectrum of Life 13

    6. Setting Your intentions 17

    7. Your Bucket List 21

    8. Goal Setting 25

    9. Create Your Why 27

    10. Formula For Change 31

    11. Create Your Identity 37

    12. Mindset for challenging times 41

    13. Success Habits 49

    14. Discipline 55

    15. Making Your Vision Board 57

    16. More Success Strategies 65

Final Thoughts 71

Gratitude & Thanks 73

Bibliography 75

Professional Development Options With Karen 77

More Books & Publications By Karen Tui Boyes 79

INTRODUCTION

I have been creating vision boards for at least 16 years for myself, my relationship with my husband and with our children.

It started in 2002. I was running two businesses, had a team of people I was responsible for, a two-and-a-half year boy and a new born daughter. Oh and a husband! I had been awarded the title of NZ Business Woman of the Year in 2001 and I thought I was invincible. I was travelling the country with our new baby, presenting at conferences, schools and conducting workshops. My Dad travelled with us and he would look after the baby while I worked, bringing her to me in the breaks for feeding. My beautiful, blue eyed baby would sleep most of the day with her grandfather and wake every two hours for feeding at night. I was exhausted. During presentations, I would start a sentence and have no idea how I was going to finish it. Making simple decisions – potatoes mashed or roasted – seemed too hard to answer. Every day people would tell me how amazing I was, how inspired they were by me and inside I was lost, unsure about myself, my relationship and my children.

Looking back now, it is likely I was going through some form of postnatal depression, except no one knew – least of all me. I did not know how to ask for help, I was a strong independent woman. Everyone, including those closest to me, just expected me to be strong.

I hit rock bottom late 2002. I had packed my bags and was leaving my husband and children. I stood at the door, not knowing where I was going, and my husband, through his tears, asked me to stay. We sat on the steps and talked. It was the first time, in a long while that I felt heard. We agreed to take life one day at a time. To re-evaluate each day. I asked him if we could make a vision board about our relationship and family. He agreed. We sat around the table with magazines and talked about our goals for us as a couple, what we wanted for our children and our future. It was uplifting and liberating. We suddenly had a shared vision and I had a clear purpose in front of me.

For the next ten years, my husband and I created a vision board together on either New Year's Eve or New Year's Day. (We had young children and were not the party type – truth be known we were likely to have been in bed before 10pm!)

Our children started creating boards a couple of years later. Our daughter was two years old and she cut out (well ripped!) pictures of magazines of ice creams and babies, her two loves at the time! When our son was in primary school, he decided he wanted an iPad so he cut a photo out and put it on his vision board. Two years later he paid for his own iPad. I believe the vision board kept him focused on his goal.

Every year I have also created a vision board for me personally. Some of this mimics our couples board, but mostly it expanded to who I wanted to become, my hobbies, personal goals and intentions.

A few years ago, I made a vision board for my business as well. I revisit this board each year and have not felt compelled to do another one yet.

After being asked by my family and friends, I started inviting people over on New Year's Day with a 2pm start for those who needed it! It was so much fun, I developed a workshop which ran in early January. After a few years of workshopping the vision boards, people asked for the workshop from further afield and I created an online live webinar style workshop. This has been incredibly successful and has had people attend from all over the world.

So, now the book! It seemed like the logical next step. I have learned so much from both a personal level and from the amazing attendees at my events.

As a thought leader, I am always highly influenced by what I am reading, listening to or watching at the time of writing. Prior to starting to write this book I joined Robin Sharma's 5am Club. I was reading *Atomic Habits*, by James Clear, and was listening to an audio book of Mark Manson's: *The Subtle Art of Not Giving a F*ck*. I also participated in a women's wellbeing retreat with Lauren Parsons.

Over the past 3 decades, I have attended a myriad of workshops, seminars, bootcamps and business schools focused on professional and personal development, read hundreds of books and tested out ideas for myself. I have had the utmost privilege of working and presenting in 20 countries and learning so much from my participants and clients.

This book contains my learnings, summaries and experiences. It is designed to be a guide, a workbook, a coach and inspiration to assist you in creating the life of your dreams. Stop talking about it and as the Nike slogan says, "Just do it!" I'm not going to guarantee this process will be easy, however I am certain it will be worth it. Take the time to stop, reflect and create. Dive in – give the exercises and activities a go and live the life you have dreamed of!

Life is not measured by the number of breaths we take, but by the moments that take our breath away.

- Maya Angelou

1 GETTING STARTED

I know I have been guilty of not doing the activities in books I have read, justifying that I simply wanted the information. It will be tempting and easy to do this with this book as well and skip straight to the fun, creative, colourful part of making your vision board. I also know that when I have taken the time to complete the questions, do the deep thinking and take time for meaningful reflection, the outcome has been much stronger and far more purposeful.

To get started, put aside three hours, just for you. I know this is hard, and it sometimes seems impossible. Make a date with yourself. Put it in your diary as an appointment with yourself. Let friends and family know you will be unavailable during that time. Gather your resources beforehand. Think about and organise the music you might play in the background. Bring your favourite nutritious snacks and drink. You might even decide to do this at a coffee shop, at a picnic table by the beach or river, or on your living room floor.

This might seem indulgent to spend three hours for yourself, but it certainly is not. It is about making you a priority, valuing yourself and designing your dream life. All successful people take time to dream, design and develop the life of their dreams. It is not selfish; it is a necessity for success.

You will spend the first half on the visioning process – thinking and designing the next stages of your life. The second half will be making a visual representation of your goals and dreams.

> *Investing in yourself is the most important investment you will ever make in your life.*
>
> - Tim Ferris

Grab your coloured pens, pencils, crayons and WRITE IN THIS BOOK! It is only recently that I have started to write in books, and it is so liberating. I have designed this book as a workbook so you can write in it. Circle parts you wish to revisit, reread and share. Make notes in the margins and record your ponderings and ideas on the pages. Complete the exercises. Draw pictures if you prefer, rather than writing the words.

If you are not sure of an answer to a question, come back to it. Dip in and out of the chapters if that is your style. The important part is the thinking, searching, pondering, and reflection you do on the way to creating your vision board. Doing the deep work will reveal your true goals and dreams. This may be confronting at times and I know, from doing it myself, and leading so many people through the process, that it is worth it.

By the way you might like to consider making vision boarding a family affair. As I mentioned in the introduction, our daughter has been doing this since she was two years old. Or make yours an inspiration for the others around you.

Most of all have fun, make it fun!

REVIEW – REFLECTING BACK

As a Sagittarian I'm always looking forward – looking for the next goal, the next idea, the next challenge. I seldom take the time to look back and reflect. However, when I do, I find it so refreshing and enlightening. It is a great way to take stock of your journey, growth and learning.

Before moving forward, take time to stop and review what has come before, the good, the bad, the ugly and importantly the lessons. This will become the basis for you to continue growing and moving in the direction you desire, rather than recreating more of the same and going around in circles.

Take a moment to reflect on these questions and record your answers below.

What are some of the great memories, actions and decisions you made in the last 12 months?

_____
_____
_____
_____
_____

What are a couple of things that did not work out so great?

_____
_____
_____
_____
_____
_____

List a few of your big lessons in the past 12 months.

_____
_____
_____
_____
_____
_____

GETTING CLEAR

There is a great scene in the movie, Alice in Wonderland, when Alice comes to the crossroads and asks the Cheshire Cat which path she should take. The Cheshire Cat replies; "That depends on where you are going." Alice replies; "I don't know." The Cheshire Cat smiles and states; "Then it does not matter which path you take."

> *It's OK if you don't have big goals and ambitions. It's OK not to have it all figured out. It's OK to not be rushing on to the next big thing.*
>
> - Joseph Campbell

Successful people do not have everything all worked out – they are often still building the aeroplane while flying it! What they do have, is a clear direction in which the plane is flying.

Getting clear on what you want and don't want is essential. International speaker & educator, Glenn Capelli tells a story about three Russian brothers Morrov, Lessov and Ridov and their cousin, Tossin.

Put on your best Russian accent and read the following questions.

- What would you like Morrov in your life?
- What would you like Lessov?

- What do you want to get Ridov?
- What might you Tossin to your life this year?

Take a moment to fill in the chart below...

What do you want 'less of' this year?	What do you want 'more of' this year?

What do you want to get 'rid of' this year?	What do you want to 'toss in' this year?

Life either happens by design or default. You choose.

- Bob Proctor

 BRAG LIST

Speaker and author Peggy Klaus' book BRAG! - *The Art of Tooting Your Horn Without Blowing It,* really appeals to me. She teaches how to achieve self-promotion and networking with grace and impact.

Living down-under in New Zealand, we have an unusual phenomenon here called the Tall Poppy Syndrome. It comes from a belief that equality and fairness are principle values and if someone seems to be more successful than the group, there is a need to discredit them and bring them 'back to our level.'

It is a particular cultural trait that sees people not want to shine too bright and make their family, friends and neighbours feel less. This is evident in most areas of our society, except in Rugby. We expect nothing but the top performance from our beloved All Blacks rugby team.

The difference is this… in many countries when the poppy farmer goes out to his field one morning and sees a poppy one metre taller than the others, she will stand there in awe and wonder how to make all her other poppies grow that tall. Conversely, a New Zealand (or Australian for that matter) poppy farmer will see a poppy one metre taller that then others and cut it down.

Celebrating your successes can seem like you are boasting, being big headed or showing off. It is key to acknowledge your successes. It is not about being ego driven. Sharing your success can be actioned in a humble way and is likely to create a positive ripple effect on others.

Achieving goals and your desires is better when you can share your successes and celebrate them. Each time you celebrate your accomplishments, you raise the bar for your next steps. It is also known to boost your confidence, help to stave off burnout and fuel your continued success. Seeing how far you have come, rather than how far you have to go, can be a prime motivating factor to keep going.

Stopping and truly experiencing the wonders and goals you have achieved creates more success.

The more you praise and celebrate your life,
the more there is in life to celebrate.

- Oprah Winfrey

Take a moment to list some of your past goals and achievements that you are proud of...

Remember to leave room to add future successes...

THE SPECTRUM OF LIFE

Life is made up of many different factors and segments. It is important to view the whole spectrum, so you can focus and work on each area. Focusing only on your financial life may have serious ramifications for your health and relationships.

You cannot focus on everything at the same time. If you decide to go north, you cannot go south simultaneously. It is useful to know your score card to set priorities and choose a direction.

Take the quiz on the next pages and rate your satisfaction level in each of the areas in your life. Get out your coloured pencils or crayons to colour the rainbow to clearly see where you are 'in flow' and which areas you might choose to work on first.

Quiz:

Rate your satisfaction on a scale from 1-10 in these 8 areas. 1 is highly dissatisfied with 10 being highly satisfied. Think about the following questions in relation to the eight areas of your life and make some notes.

- How balanced do I feel in this area of my life?
- What might be missing in this area of my life?
- Am I neglecting anything that might add value to this area of my life?

Health & Wellbeing:

How physically healthy are you? Are you satisfied with your level of fitness? Are you satisfied with your nutrition? Are you getting quality sleep? Do you have the energy you desire?

Home & Family:

Is your family supportive of you? Are you supportive of your family? Are you happy with where you live?

Work & Career:

Is your work/career where you want it to be? Are you heading in the right direction? Are you happy in your work? Do you feel productive?

Money:

Are you earning enough income to satisfy your current needs? Are you financially set up for future growth in wealth? Do you have a savings scheme?

Personal Growth:

How focused are you on personal growth? Are you satisfied with your direction? Are you trying new experiences and seeking to learn?

Friends & Social:

Are your friends supportive of you? Are you engaging friends & socialising to your satisfaction levels?

Romance:

Do you feel loved? How often are you expressing love? Are you happy with your current relationship status? (It is perfectly OK to be single, if you love being single.)

Recreation & Fun:

Are you enjoying your life and making it fun? Are you satisfied with the level of activity you do?

Now you have completed the quiz, consider which areas would be beneficial to focus on. You will set goals in these areas in the next chapter.

CREATING THE LIFE OF YOUR DREAMS

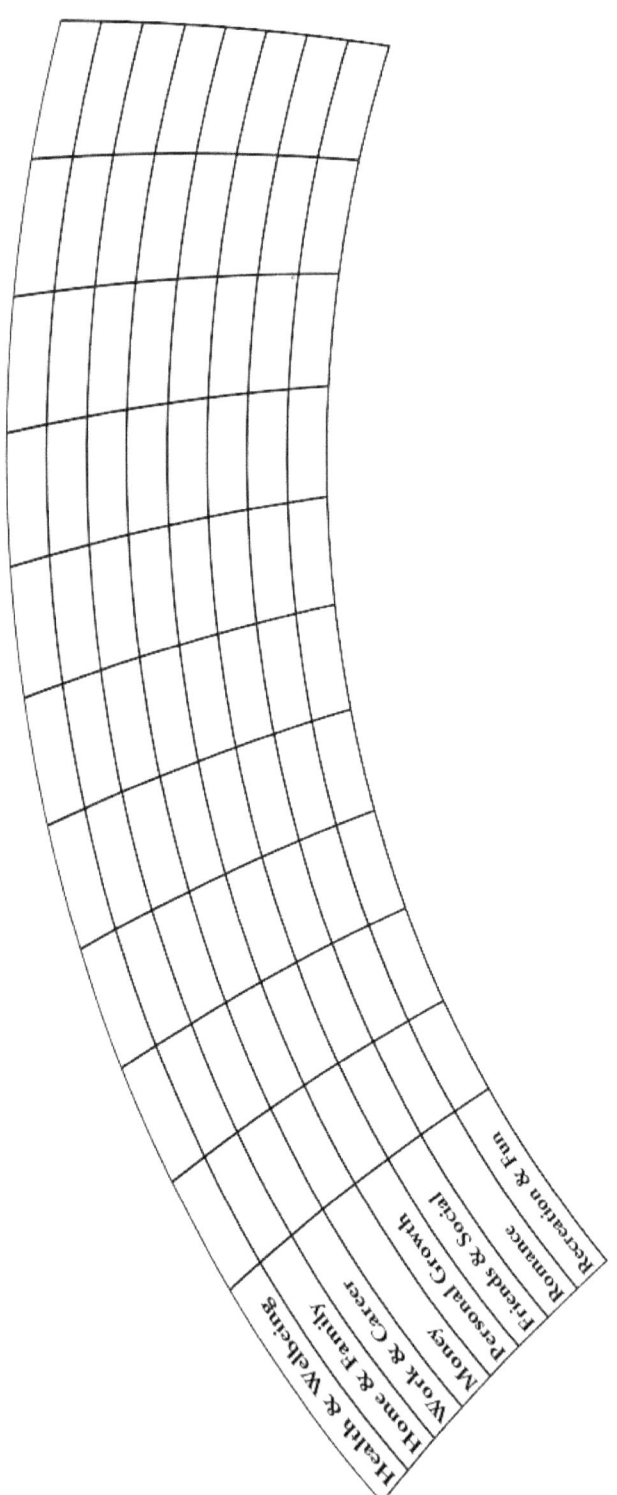

Spectrum of Life™
- getting into the rainbow flow...

16 | The Spectrum of Life

6 SETTING YOUR INTENTIONS

The clearer you are, in all areas of your life the better focus you will have. The late Reverend Ike, a famous minister from New York, teacher and speaker on joy and prosperity said;

> *You must be definite with the infinite.*
> - Reverend Ike

The clearer you are the more your brain will look for ways to attain your goals. More about this in Chapter 8.

Before you start a caution! Be careful what you ask for. A colleague was not satisfied with her romance status of being single. She said she really wanted to attract fun, kind and good looking men. She did – three of them! She only wanted one, and she really liked them all! It caused far too much stress and she stopped seeing all of them. An initial adjustment of the goal to be more specific – one man, might have helped her situation. Of course, if you think you can handle three – go for it!! ☺

Reflect on the following headings below and set some goals and intentions in some or all of these areas. Ask yourself: What do I want in the short, mid and long term?

Health & Wellbeing

_____

_____

_____

Home & Family

_____

_____

_____

Work & Career

_____

_____

_____

Money

_____

_____

_____

Personal Growth

_____

_____

_____

Friends & Social Life

_____
_____
_____

Romance

_____
_____
_____

Recreation & Fun

_____
_____
_____

Other

_____
_____
_____

Just as your car runs more smoothly and requires less energy to go faster and farther when the wheels are in perfect alignment, you perform better when your thoughts, feelings, emotions, goals, and values are in balance.

- Brian Tracy

7 YOUR BUCKET LIST

Have you seen the movie *The Bucket List* featuring Jack Nicholson and Morgan Freeman? If not, put it on your goal list! It's essentially about not waiting until you are on your death bed and feeling regretful about what you coulda, woulda or shoulda done in your life, and instead, doing them now! Imagine planning a life plan that allows you to look back at the end of your days and feel totally fulfilled and satisfied.

Travis Bell is the world's number one Bucket List expert and is committed to helping people live their bucket lists before it is too late. He teaches people to focus on what they want and to achieve big things. You can find out more about Travis' work here: www.thebucketlistguy.com

Travis talks about the fact that ticking off items is not only about the items on your list – it is more about who you become in the process and how you can positively influence others on you journey.

He shared with me his 12 steps to creating a Bucket List and has given me permission to share it with you. ☺ Thanks Trav!

Take some time to brainstorm some of the experiences, learnings and actions you would like in the future…

MY BUCKET LIST ™ Travis Bell

M = Meet a personal hero: Who do you want to meet, take out for dinner, spend time with?

Y = Your proud achievements: When you look back on your life what do you want to be proud of?

B = Buy that special something: It might be for you or someone else.

U = Ultimate challenge: What would move you way outside your comfort zone and show you that you have more potential than you thought?

C = Conquer a fear: What scares you that you wish it didn't?

K = Kind acts for others: What can you do at a local, national or global level? How can you give back?

E = Express yourself: What have you stopped doing which lit you up? Are you honouring the creative part of you?

T = Take lessons: What skills do you want to learn?

L = Leave a legacy: Big stuff here! How would you like to be remembered and/or how will your work continue once you have gone?

I = Idiotic stuff: Embrace the fun stuff, spontaneity and the silly.

S = Satisfy a Curiosity: What would you like to taste, touch, smell, see, experience?

T = Travel adventures: Be a tourist in your own town, country, continent or internationally.

Brainstorm your ideas in the box below.

CREATING THE LIFE OF YOUR DREAMS

This is about the person you have the potential to become in the process & the effect you'll have on your circle of influence.

— Travis Bell

If you are clear about your goals and take the right direction every day, eventually you will succeed. So, decide what it is you want, write it down, review it constantly, and each day do something that moves you towards those goals.

- Jack Canfield

 GOAL SETTING

The research is very clear. Setting goals is good for you! Having a strong set of goals improves performance, increases your motivation to achieve, improves self-confidence, and increases your personal pride and satisfaction of the finished product or outcome.

There are three main types of goals you might set. These are long term goals, mid term goals and short term goals.

Long term goals are focused on the end game, the big picture or something you want to do or be in the future, whether 2-3 years from now or 10-15 years away. They are fundamental for a successful career and life. A long term goal requires planning and time. Breaking your long term goals into smaller mid and short term timeframes will help you achieve the long term goal that you ultimately desire.

Naturally, mid term goals and short term goals are achieved over a shorter time span and are more quickly attainable. Usually, a mid term goal spans over a two month to a three year timeframe. Examples might include term or half year goals. A short term goal is something you want to achieve today, this week or within the next two months. Often short term goals are small steps towards a mid or long term goal. Both mid term and short term goals should align with the long term goal and what you are hoping to achieve.

While you are setting your goals and designing what you would like to achieve there are some key factors to ensuring your goal setting is successful.

Going PRO:

P= Positive: Ensure you state your goals using positive words. What you focus on is what you get. Are you focused on what you want or the opposite? Frame your goals in terms of what you DO want to achieve. Instead of, "I don't want to fail my test," say, "I will pass my test with ease."

R = Realistic: Richard Branson and Bill Gates say if you want to change the world, set a goal that is unrealistic and then work towards making it happen. However, if you are not aiming that big just yet, setting goals that are realistic is recommended. This means being specific about what you want to do and choosing something that is attainable within the time frame you have set. If you cannot swim, being chosen for the swim team this summer is not likely to be a realistic goal. However it could be if you work towards it in the long term. Having a benchmark of where you are at now will help with this. Take stock of your current skills and abilities and be honest with yourself. Now set a goal in a timeframe that you are willing to work for. Persistence, focus and hard work will be required so your goal must be worth the effort.

O= Objectives: Break your bigger goals into small achievable steps. This helps create the feeling of achievement, which in turn gives you small wins and increases your motivation to keep achieving. You may have many steps towards a goal. The clearer the pathway the easier it is to take each step towards completing your goals. Having a mentor or a coach might also be useful. It might be a family member, colleague or a friend who is willing to hold you accountable.[1]

---

[1] Remember to ask for help from people who have walked the path you are on. For example, if you are looking for relationship advice, it might be more advantageous to ask someone who has been happily married for 40 years, rather than someone divorced three times. Similarly, if you want advice about money, ask someone who is wealthy rather than someone who is struggling to feed their family.

9 CREATE YOUR "WHY?"

Knowing your 'why' is paramount for success. Simon Sinek's best selling books, *Start With Why* and *Find Your Why*, both outline the importance of starting here.

He calls it his Golden Circles. Great companies and people, Simon explains, are clear on their 'why' which drives the how and the what.

Reasons come first, answers come second.
- Jim Rohn

There is a big difference between knowing how to ride a bike and having a reason – or a 'why' to ride your bike. Knowing your why will assist with motivation, focus and taking action.

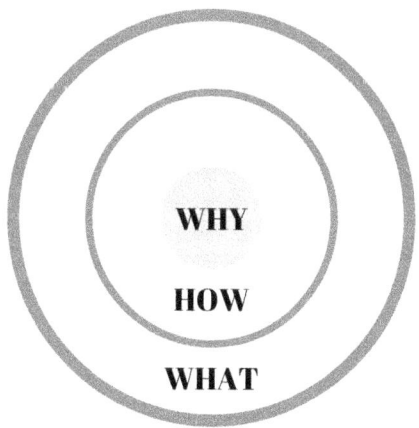

Your why is your compass for making decisions. There are so many unknowns when pursuing anything new. Having a purpose will help steer you towards doing the few key actions to move you forward.

Your why also needs to be heart centred and bigger than you. These are the reasons you must absolutely have and achieve these goals no matter what. Imaginehaving already achieved your goals and why these successes are important.

Choose your top three goals, from previous chapters, and write a paragraph of your why's. Paint a clear picture. Record how it will make you and others feel and what you would be saying to yourself when you are successful. Why is this crucial to you?

Goal 1:

_____
_____
_____
_____
_____
_____

Goal 2:

_____
_____
_____
_____
_____
_____

Goal 3:

_____

_____

_____

_____

_____

_____

Don't wish it was easier, wish you were better. Don't wish for less problems, wish for more skills. Don't wish for less challenges, wish for more wisdom.

- Jim Rohn

FORMULA FOR CHANGE

Yes! There is a formula for everything it seems. I first learned the formula for change from entrepreneur Brad Sugars.

Personal Change Formula: D x V x F > R

D = Dissatisfaction
V = Vision
F = First steps
R = Resistance

Essentially what this means is, to create change you first need some dissatisfaction. If everything is going well in your life and you are happy with your direction, then you will have no reason to do something different. Secondly, you need a vision – a goal or outcome that looks attractive to you and thirdly, you require some idea of the first steps to take. These three factors must be greater than your resistance or your need to stay the same.

Advertisers often use this formula. They build your dissatisfaction with your life, share a vision of how your life could be, and then promote a product or service to cater to you being able to take action. If they are convincing enough, and make the purchase easy with... a call this freecall number now, or 3 easy small payments, or order now, pay later etc, and if your resistance to the change is small, you will place your order.

Think about cleaning products. Growing up my Mum used Ajax powder to clean the bathroom and kitchen stainless steel. She had to rub, scrub, rinse and polish. Then came the 'Spray n Wipe' products. Advertisers sold consumers on the idea that it would be quicker and more efficient, and the result would be more time to do the things they really wanted. Enter the 60 Seconds products and the catch phrase, 'Spray and Walk Away!' The illusion increased our dissatisfaction with our current products as this product would make our life so much better!

One of the places to start when visioning your year or life is to consider what you are dissatisfied with, create the vision of what you do want, and then create/learn/design the first steps to get your momentum.

Once you have done this, wellbeing specialist, Lauren Parsons, says you must FOWYW. This stands for Focus On What You Want. She goes on to say, "Because of our negativity bias, we naturally focus on what we don't want – on our problems and challenges – and this is where we get stuck." For example: I don't want to be overweight. I don't want to be in my current job. I don't want to be fighting with my children. I don't want to be worrying about money. The list goes on.

The challenge with this 'don't' thinking is the brain is unable to recognise the word don't. Give this a go:

>Don't think of yellow.

>Don't think of a purple cat.

>Don't think of that purple cat in a pink tree.

What did you think of? Yellow, a purple cat and a pink tree? This is because your brain is unable to initially recognise the word 'don't.' Firstly, your brain has to think of the colour yellow and secondarily think, 'I'm not supposed to think of that! It is already too late. You are focused on the yellow.

Consider some of the phrases we may use each day.

- Don't touch
- Don't worry
- Don't leave it until the last minute
- Don't eat unhealthy food
- Don't drink and drive
- Don't forget

In the next week, take notice of how many 'don't' phrases you hear yourself or others use. See if you can avoid the 'don't' phrases and replace them with a positive phrase that describes what you do want.

Your actions tend to line up with what you've been focusing on. Are you focusing on what you don't want or do what? As Lauren advocates "Focus On What You Want."

Alternative phrases to those above, focusing on the positive outcome, include;

- ~~Don't touch~~ - Keep your hands to yourself
- ~~Don't worry~~ - Stay calm
- ~~Don't leave it until the last~~ minute - Do a little bit a day
- ~~Don't eat unhealthy food~~ - Eat healthy food
- ~~Don't drink and drive~~ – Drive sober
- ~~Don't forget~~ - Remember

How does this work?

You have an amazing part of the brain called the Reticular Activating System, or the RAS. Its job is to let important information into your brain, like a giant filter. What your brain deems as important is often what you spend the most time focusing on, whether good or bad. Your RAS confirms your beliefs and biases. If you have a belief that parenting is hard work, your RAS will notice the information, situations and experiences to prove this thought. However, if you think parenting is a privilege, your RAS will notice, record and recall instances of this.

It's like an internal GPS that you are constantly programming to lead you in a certain direction, whether you realise it or not. Think about the last time you bought a new car. Most likely once you started researching and test driving that car and finally bought it, you will have started to see that make and model of car more and more often. There aren't more models on the road, you're just noticing them because your RAS is highlighting them to you, because you've spent time thinking about that car.

If you want to start a business, suddenly you'll notice business funding on billboards or online. If you want to be a better parent, you'll notice other parents' words and techniques. If you want to re-landscape your garden, everywhere you go you'll notice the plants that work well in light and in shade.

Whatever you focus on starts to direct your actions because your RAS highlights things in line with those thoughts.

Give this a go:

> Look around the room and notice at least 10 things that are red... go.
>
> Now close your eyes and recall everything you saw that was...

... green.

How did you get on recalling all the green? While you are focusing on red, it is hard to see the green. In the same way, when you focus on what you don't want, you miss the opportunities for what you want to happen.

The 20 Second Barrier

Once you have the vision of what you would like, developing small steps, the first step is imperative. James Clear, in his book, *Atomic Habits*, discussed the 20 second barrier which often stops us from moving forward.

Here is an example. My birthday was ten months ago. One of my good friends gave me a gift which required hanging on the wall. I knew exactly where I was going to hang the gift and simply needed to find six small nails to complete the task. This was my 20 second barrier. I knew or had a fairly good idea of where the nails would be, yet this barrier stopped me for ten months! I would walk past the gift on my dressing table and say to myself, "I need to hand that up." While reading about the 20 second barrier, it hit me... it would take 20 seconds to find the nails, and once I had, the job was easy. And it was! My gift now hangs on my wall. It took 20 seconds! What 20 second barrier is holding you back from moving forward?

To create these first steps, consider what you can do to get started. If you want to eat a healthy breakfast, get it ready before you go to bed. If you choose to exercise in the morning, place your exercise gear beside your bed so you can get into it as soon as you get out of bed.

Jot down some of your goals below and add the first steps you might take to break down the 20 second barrier.

Goal is _____

And my first step will be_____

_____

Goal is _____

And my first step will be _____

_____

Goal is _____

And my first step will be _____

To revise, the formula for change is D x V x F > R and your **D**issatisfaction, **V**ision and **F**irst steps must be bigger than the **R**esistance you are putting up to prevent you achieving your goals.

CREATE YOUR IDENTITY

Be – Do – Have is a phrase that I learned many years ago at a workshop. The presenter talked about who do you need to BE in order to DO what you need to do to receive what you would like to HAVE.

This is about your identity. When working towards changing a habit or toward a particular goal, it is paramount to align who you are with the goal. This takes time and often deep reflection into your beliefs.

For example, if your goal is to be rich and you believe rich people are mean, you are likely to sabotage your efforts toward gaining wealth, assuming you want to remain a kind person. Understanding that money amplifies a person's personality is key for this goal. If a person is mean to start with, money is likely to create more meanness. If they are generous before coming into money, it is highly likely they will be even more generous with money. I know many wealthy people who give millions away for positive impact in the world.

If your goal is to stop smoking, your identity will play a role here too. If you tell people you have not had a cigarette for five days, your identity is one of a smoker. Changing your identity to a non-smoker is a major key to success here.

When I wanted to be healthier and more vibrant, I needed to change my identity from someone who frequently ate sweet treats and deserved them because I work hard, to someone who does not eat between meals and eats balanced and healthy meals three times a day.

Who do you need to BE to set yourself up for success?

Rowena McEvoy, co-founder of the Max College of Fitness, tells a story which goes like this.

> Imagine you are at work and a detective comes into town with a mission to find out 'who' you are. She has a photograph of you and knows some of the local places you frequent. Armed with the photograph and a notebook, the detective visits the petrol station, supermarket, shopping mall and hairdresser you go to, and inquires about you. She writes down the words people use to describe you. What do you think they might say?
>
> She then goes to your home. As no-one is home, she carefully breaks in. She looks around looking for clues as to who you are. Next she opens your pantry and fridge and examines the food you eat. Are the dishes left on the bench? Is there rubbish on the floor? Next she makes her way into your bedroom. Is the bed made? Are your clothes hung up? She looks under the bed, in your closet and notes down the words that describe your habits.

Whist this seems very invasive, and it is just a story, it illustrates that who we are in public may be different to who we are in private. Who is the real you? Whatever your answer to this question, stay calm. We are all a work in progress. I can personally vouch for the fact that if you came into my house unannounced, there will be dust on the coffee table, tiny cobwebs in some corners and my teens shoes and socks left on the lounge room floor!

The point is to take some time and think about who you want to be. What is your ideal identity?

There are over 600 words in the dictionary that define a person's positive qualities. Scan a selection of these below.

Circle or highlight the ones you are, and the ones you would like to be.

List of Personal Qualities

I am...	Far-sighted	Methodical
Academic	Forceful	Meticulous
Accurate	Formal	Mild
Active	Frank	Moderate
Adaptable	Generous	Modest
Adventurous	Gentle	Natural
Affectionate	Good-natured	Obliging
Alert	Healthy	Opportunistic
Ambitious	Helpful	Optimistic
Broadminded	Honest	Organised
Business like	Humorous	Original
Conservative	Imaginative	Outgoing
Courageous	Independent	Painstaking
Curious	Individualistic	Patient
Daring	Industrious	Persevering
Determined	Informal	Pleasant
Dignified	Intellectual	Polite
Discreet	Intelligent	Practical
Dominant	Inventive	Precise
Eager	Kind	Progressive
Easy-going	Leisurely	Prudent
Emotional	Light-hearted	Purposeful
Energetic	Loyal	Realistic
Fair	Mature	Reflective

Relaxed	Stable	Unaffected
Reliable	Steady	Unassuming
Resourceful	Strong	Understanding
Responsible	Strong-minded	Uninhibited
Retiring	Tactful	Versatile
Robust	Teachable	Wholesome
Self-controlled	Tenacious	Wise
Sensible	Thorough	Witty
Sincere	Thoughtful	Zany
Sociable	Tolerant	
Spontaneous	Trusting	
Spunky	Trustworthy	

Which personal assets and qualities of character would you need/have to assist you in achieving your goals?

Choose five (yes, you can have six if you must!) words to focus on this year and focus on them as if they are true already. You will add these to your vision board.

I am…

1 _____

2 _____

3 _____

4 _____

5 _____

 MINDSET FOR CHALLENGING TIMES

Challenges will always come up when you are heading towards your goals. They are a test to see how serious you are to reach your goals.

> *Believe in yourself and all that you are. Know that there is something inside you that is greater than any obstacle.*
>
> — Christian Larson

Take some time to think about and plan how you might deal with these events.

Developing a mindset for success is essential, which includes how you will deal with the failures and disappointments.

One of the most powerful frameworks I was taught is the Responsibility Chart. In a nutshell, it operates on the idea that you always have choice. You may not have control over an actual event, such as a car crash, earthquake, or some else's behaviour but you do have control and choice over how you respond.

There are two main choices. When something goes wrong, you make a mistake, or your result was not as you expected, you have the option to respond above or below the line. To play the game of life on the Victim Team or the Learning Team.

People who 'play below the line' will often blame, make excuses and deny their actions, mistakes, outcomes, etc. This causes them to miss out on the learning opportunity from that situation. Below the line comments include:

- It was his fault
- I haven't got time
- I had nothing to do with it
- They made me do it
- This is stupid

People who 'play above the line,' look for the learning opportunity by taking ownership of their results, become accountable for their actions and responsible for their outcomes. This is where growth, learning and refining your life comes from. Above the line comments include:

- I made a mistake and need to fix that
- I hurt my partner's feelings by not listening fully and need to apologise
- I didn't express my ideas and am not happy with the direction we are going. I need to call a team meeting
- It's my fault for not managing my time well

We are all human and it is normal to blame, make excuses and deny. The critical factor is recognising when you are below the line and reframing the challenge or situation to the position of the learning team - above the line.

In any situation you can choose to be a victim or a learner – you can't be both!

Planning to Fail

If failure is a master teacher, why is it not part of our plan?

- Dr Fatma Odaymat

Pre-empting challenges and failure, and designing ways to cope and combat these, can be a useful strategy towards success. Social entrepreneur, Roger Hamilton talks about planning to fail or what psychologists call implementation intentions. It is a simple idea, which comes down to knowing ahead of time exactly what you'll do if you veer off course. Rather than quitting, you might develop some 'if-then' responses.

For example, let's say one of your goals is to eat healthy nutritious food. It is possible you will go out for dinner and be faced with many options, not all aligned with your goal. Decide ahead of time your course of action. For example, '<u>If</u> we go out for dinner, <u>then</u> I will order a salad instead of the fries.'

Or maybe your goal is to get fit and you plan to go for a daily run. This is easier when the weather is fine and warm, or crisp and clear. What will you do when it is raining and cold? Your pre-planning may include, '<u>If</u> it is raining, <u>then</u> I will wear a raincoat.' Alternatively, '<u>If</u> it is raining, <u>then</u> I will run up and down the stairs in my home for 20 minutes instead.'

Benjamin Hardy, in his article *How Planning To Fail Can Help You Succeed*, states, "Because planning to act on a goal, even if that goal describes what you do when you *fa*il, actually can create a clearer and more accurate cognitive picture about that future situation. That clarity persists until your plan is enacted or your goal achieved."

Give this a go… consider three of your goals and plan what you will do if a negative situation occurs.

My goal is to _____

If _____ (a negative situation) **happens, then I will**
_____ (solution or alternative action)

My goal is to _____

If _____ (a negative situation) **happens, then I will**
_____ (solution or alternative action)

My goal is to _____

If _____ (a negative situation) happens, then I will
_____ (solution or alternative action)

The Two Minute Rule

In his book, *Atomic Habits*, James Clear talks about adopting a two minute rule. He suggests boiling a new habit or routine, into something that takes less than two minutes to do. All habits can be scaled down to a two minute version that will get you started and help you succeed. James' list includes:

"Read before bed each night," becomes "Read one page"

"Do 20 minutes of yoga," becomes "Unroll my yoga mat on the floor."

"Fold the laundry" becomes, "Fold one t-shirt."

Once you get started, momentum will often keep you moving forward.

Create a Support Team

Successful people have a team of supporters in the background. Seeking support to achieve your goals is essential. You do not have to, nor should you, do this alone.

> *If you want to go fast, go alone. If you want to go far, go together."*
>
> \- African Proverb.

Having cheerleaders in your corner certainly helps. Who might coach and support you? While family members often seem like a great idea, I personally avoid laying my success on them. It is often far too easy to fob them off, make excuses and even blame them for your lack of progress. I usually look for people outside my immediate circle. Over the years I have worked closely with personal trainers, business coaches and health professionals to keep me on track. It does not have to be a face-to-face, online support can be equally effective. Enrol in an online course, join a support group of like-minded people (on or offline), go on a retreat, a business school course, enrol in a seminar, etc.

Publicly announcing your goals can often add pressure to succeed. When writing my last book, I put self-imposed dates on my timeline and kept myself accountable by advertising the book to clients for pre-sale, before I had even finished it. Those first few orders were not only affirming of my topic and ideas, knowing people were interested in them gave me the momentum to keep moving so as not to disappoint the early supporters. Perhaps, it works as some form of reverse psychology. One of the worst thoughts I had was having to contact all my supporters who had pre-paid for the book and tell them that I had not done it! Wanting to avoid this, I ensured the book was completed.

The Mother-In-Law Factor

This might also be a useful strategy to use. With the upmost respect to my late mother-in-law, she was a no nonsense woman who I was a little timid around when I first met my husband. She was great for my motivation! I would tell her a goal I had set or a project I was working on and every time I saw her, she would ask, "Have you done it yet?" The fear of saying 'no' to her kept me focused. Maybe if there is not a mother-in-law in your life that could do this, who might be that person who would constantly remind you of your promises and keep you on track?

> *You must accept that you might fail; then, if you do your best and still don't win, at least you can be satisfied that you've tried. If you don't accept failure as a possibility, you don't set high goals, you don't branch out, you don't try - you don't take the risk.*
>
> - Rosalynn Carter

Take a moment to plan for the unexpected and challenging times. Ask yourself these questions and record some of your ideas and strategies below.

- Will you play above or below the line of life?
- Who might support you in your quest to achieve your goals?
- What might you need to STOP doing in order to achieve your goals?
- Are you willing to fail?
- When the roadblocks appear, how will you best handle these?

_____

_____

_____

_____

_____

_____

_____

_____

_____

What you get by achieving your goals is not as important as what you become by achieving your goals.

- Henry David Thoreau

SUCCESS HABITS

One of my favourite quotes from Robin Sharma, author of *The 5AM Club: Own Your Morning. Elevate Your Life,* is,

> *Successful people are willing do what unsuccessful people will not.*
>
> - Robin Sharma

Take time to consider what you are willing and not willing to do to achieve the life of your dreams.

Everything is Hard Before it is Easy

"To get to easy you have to go through hard." This was a soft drink commercial on the back of a bus and on billboards in Wellington, New Zealand.

A great goal is going to stretch and challenge you beyond what you have done before. And it is going to get hard.

It is easy to look at others achieving their goals and think it is fun and easy. It is not always! Sometimes it is uncomfortable, awkward and that feeling of potential failure is something most of us like to avoid. However, this is exactly what learning new and unfamiliar habits feels like. When learning and life becomes hard, many people give up. Again, the key is, as the advert says, "To get to easy, you have to go through hard."

When you are stuck or just don't know what to do, it is useful to have anticipated this and have reflected upon possible solutions.

In life, we often start on our journey with a goal in mind, a plan of perfection. In reality the journey is frequently very bumpy. It is, however, in those bumps, those challenging times, where the best learning often happens.

Being paralysed with fear of failing and making mistakes is not something you want. It is in the making of mistakes, the failing, the bumpiness, where life feels unfair, that sometimes the best learning and growth happens.

Getting Unstuck

When you find yourself stuck and not sure what to do, consider using strategies such as to persist, try again and keep going.

> *If Plan A doesn't work, there are 25 more letters in the alphabet!*

Two people who have thought a great deal about this, are Professor Art Costa and Dr Bena Kallick. They studied, founded and developed the 16 Habits of Mind. These are the behaviours of intelligent people and what they do when they are stuck, when the answer is not immediately apparent, and when they are not sure how to move from the hard to the easy.

A summary of the 16 Habits of Mind are below. As you read through the list, consider which dispositions or Habits will benefit you to learn and adopt while pursuing your goals, dreams and the life you crave.

1. **Persisting:** *Stick to it!* Persevering in task through to completion; remaining focused. Looking for ways to reach your goal when stuck. Not giving up.

2. **Managing Impulsivity:** *Take your time!* Thinking before acting; remaining calm, thoughtful and deliberative.

3. **Listening with Understanding and Empathy**: *Understand others!* Devoting mental energy to another person's thoughts and ideas; Making an effort to perceive another's point of view and emotions.

4. **Thinking Flexibly:** *Look at it another way!* Being able to change perspectives, generating alternatives, considering options.

5. **Thinking about Thinking (Metacognition):** *Know your knowing!* Being aware of your own thoughts, strategies, feelings and actions and their effects on others.

6. **Striving for Accuracy:** *Check it again!* Always doing your best. Setting high standards. Checking and finding ways to improve constantly.

7. **Questioning and Posing Problems:** *How do you know?* Having a questioning attitude; Knowing what data are needed & developing questioning strategies to produce those data. Finding problems to solve.

8. **Applying Past Knowledge to New Situations**: *Use what you learn!* Accessing prior knowledge; transferring knowledge beyond the situation in which it was learned

9. **Thinking and Communicating with Clarity and Precision:** *Be clear!* Striving for accurate communication in both written and oral form; Avoiding over-generalisations, distortions, deletions and exaggerations.

10. **Gathering Data through All Senses:** *Use your natural pathways!* Paying attention to the world around you. Gathering data through all the senses: Taste, touch, smell, hearing and sight.

11. **Creating, Imagining, Innovating**: *Try a different way!* Generating new and novel ideas, fluency, originality

12. **Responding with Wonderment and Awe:** *Have fun figuring it out!* Finding the world awesome, mysterious and being intrigued with phenomena and beauty.

13. **Taking Responsible Risks:** *Venture out!* Being adventuresome; living on the edge of one's competence.
    Try new things constantly.

14. **Finding Humour:** *Laugh a little!* Finding the whimsical, incongruous and unexpected. Being able to laugh at one's self.

15. **Thinking Interdependently:** *Work together!* Being able to work in and learn from others in reciprocal situations. Team work.

16. **Remaining Open to Continuous Learning:** *Learn from experiences!* Having humility and pride when admitting we don't know. Resisting complacency.

For more information about the 16 Habits of Mind, please go to www.instituteforhabitsofmind.com

Obviously, these Habits are lifelong learning tools which are important in all areas of your life. The great news is if you see some gaps in your toolbox, these behaviours can be learned and developed.

Brainstorm a list of strategies to employ when you are stuck and are faced with hard or difficult. It is a great idea to have these listed on a post it note in your diary or on the fridge to regularly remind you that there are many options to help you become unstuck, rather than giving up on your dreams.

Writing Success Statements

Now take a moment to turn your brainstormed strategies into success statements. These will be great to add to your vision board.

1. **Get personal:** Use 'I' to tell your brain it is you you are referring to. "I am healthy and vibrant." "I create positive and long lasting relationships."

2. **Be positive:** Focus on what you want – not what you don't want. Rather than saying or writing "I am not going to quit'" use, "I am persistent." Instead of saying, I'm fearful of making mistakes," say, "I am a responsible risk taker."

3. **Use the present tense:** Write and say your statements as if they are true already. Saying, "I will be…" is in the future. Consider this idea. I have heard many people say, "I will be happy when I leave school." They leave school.

"I will be happy when I get a job." They get a job. "I will be happy when I get married." They get married. "I will be happy when I have children." They have children. "I will be happy when the kids leave home…" You get the picture… the happiness is always deferred to somewhere in the future. Choose to be happy now. Use "I am…" present focused statements.

4. **Take action:** Of course, all this positive thinking does not work without appropriate action. You cannot sit on the couch every day and say, "I'm getting fit" or go to the garden every day and think, "It is weed free." Taking action in the direction of your goals and dreams is required.

Record your success statements here:

14 DISCIPLINE

Achieving your goals takes commitment and discipline. It takes focus and courage.

Discipline is the bridge between goals and accomplishment

\- Jim Rohn

There are two types of pain in goal setting – the pain of discipline or the pain of regret. Successful people choose the pain of discipline. They are willing to do what others won't.

Robin Sharma, author of *The 5am Club: Own Your Morning. Elevate Your Life* shares research from the University College London that it takes 66 days to install long term change into your life. The first 22 days are hard, where you have to let go of the old habits, practices and beliefs. Most people give up during this stage and the key is to keep going, reset, try again and accept small failures as learning opportunities. The next 22 days are messy as you create new neuro pathways. As you are now installing the new habit, confusion and exhaustion may set in. You may hear conflicting information and others may challenge your decision to change your routines and behaviour. I love the idea that obstacles are nothing more that tests designed to measure how seriously you want the rewards! It then takes a further 22 days to create 'automaticity.' In this last phase you move from hard to easy and you know it is becoming a habit when it is easier to do it, than not to do it.

> *Change is hard at the start, messy in the middle and gorgeous at the end.*
>
> - Robin Sharma

Most of all it takes discipline. If your internal voice just told you that you are not disciplined, ensure you add this as a success statement or to your five identity words and add it to your vision board.

Set a Monthly Focused Goal

The first of each month is a great opportunity to refocus your life, and create a monthly challenge.

Set a focus for the month. It could be:

- drinking more water
- no snacking between meals
- being processed sugar free
- an alcohol free month
- exercise for 10-20 minutes each morning
- only push the snooze button once
- do a short morning meditation
- Watch a TED talk each day
- Write for 30 minutes every day

Start with ONE idea, install it until it is a habit and then add another goal.

 MAKING YOUR VISION BOARD

Finally, you are here! If you have skipped straight to this page, consider going back and doing some of the thinking and reflection to really clarify your goals, dreams and desires. It will take time and it is worth it!

If you have been through all the exercises, congratulations! You are already more successful than most!

Now you have spent the time thinking, reflecting and designing how you would like your life to be, it is time to make a visual representation of this. A vision board.

> *You want to create an image of the future – a tangible representation of your dreams, goals and ideal life.*
>
> - Jack Canfield

The idea here is to work on portraying the experiences, the feelings and the possessions you desire. The goal is to visually showcase your key words, identity, bucket list goals, your *Spectrum of Life* ™, everything you have designed and created in this book.

A picture is worth a thousand words[2] is the idea that complex ideas can be conveyed with just a single picture and this picture transfers its meaning or essence more effectively than a written description does.

---

[2] As an interesting aside, according to Wikipedia, Henrik Ibsen, a Norwegian playwright and theatre director, first said "A thousand words leave not the same deep impression as does a single deed." After his death in 1906 this quote was plagiarised and para-phrased into what we know now. (Totally off topic and a fun fact for your next dinner party!)

Your mind responds strongly to visual stimulation. Did you know the human body has a staggering eleven million sensory receptors and ten million of these are for sight!

You need:

- Old magazines (opportunity or second hand shops are great for these)
- Photos, pictures, words printed from the internet (optional)
- Scissors
- Glue
- Backing paper, card or a canvas. You might even use an old notice board or the back of an old folder. I've even seen this done on a paper plate! I recommend your backing to be A4 or A3 size, and of course it can be bigger! Anything goes!
- You can choose to make your board on a computer using a graphics programme or on a blank document.

Instructions

This is not a recipe to be followed precisely. The instructions here are merely suggestions to get you thinking, creating and moving forward. In fact, most times this is a very non-linear process. If you have a time limit, I recommend that you put a timer on for searching through magazines and the internet. It can be like Alice in Wonderland, falling down a rabbit hole where you find yourself reading articles, trying to find a better picture and eventually coming back to the one you started with! Most of all have fun, enjoy the process and create your dreams.

1. Decide on a Theme for Your Board

Is it about you, your relationship/family, your business/career? Of course, you can have all of these on one board and that is perfectly fine. Do you have a central theme of your goals/ life/ vision? This may become clearer as you find pictures and sort through your goals and ideas.

2. Start With Your Central Theme

Once you have this theme, look for an image or a word to encapsulate this and place this in the centre of the board. The reason this central image is used is because the brain places key ideas in the middle position.

> Activity: Close your eyes and imagine an apple – where on the TV screen of your mind does your brain put the apple? For most people it is in the middle. It is the natural starting point for the brain.

3. Orientation: Landscape or Portrait?

This may or may not be important to you and has sometimes been a small frustration of mine. I have designed the vision board and then realised the orientation was not the way I'd like it. Consider where you are going to display it? If you want to have it as a screen saver on your phone, portrait might be best. If you wish to use it as the background on your computer, use landscape. It may not matter – so just go with the flow.

4. Search for Pictures, Words and Quotes

Start cutting, choosing pictures, phrases, quotes from magazines or download and print from the internet. You might like to use a happy photo of you and possibly your family. I have found it increasingly hard to find a Mum, Dad and two children photo in magazines!

5. Add your Five Identity Words

Add your five words by either finding them in a magazine, cutting out the letters from magazines, printing the words out or using crafting or scrapbooking letters. Remember to add any other motivational words or inspiring quotes.

6. Layout Your board

If you have chosen to have several ideas for your dream life displayed on your board, create sections on the board, fanning out from your central image. Keep it neat. Avoid creating a cluttered board as this portrays chaos and you do not want to attract chaos into your life! Avoid blank spaces on your board. Back fill spaces with pictures which are in line with your dreams, even if you don't really see them, your subconscious mind knows they are there. Simple is better than cluttered and if you have too much on the board, simply make two boards, by segmenting the categories or use a larger backing card. Be creative and add your personality.

7. Make it Stick – Make it Permanent

Once you have laid it out, take a photo with your phone so you can remember where everything was placed on the board. Often when you move everything to glue, it is hard to recall where you had placed the pictures and words. Now glue your creation to the backing board or card.

8. Record the Date

Add the date you created the board on the back and perhaps your brainstormed notes and ideas. I love looking at these notes and brainstorms a year or two down the track.

9. Display Your Board

Display your board somewhere you will see it every day. The bedroom wall, bathroom mirror, on the fridge etc. Take a photo of it and use it as a screen saver on your phone and computer. Print out the photo and add it to the inside of your diary or journal, on your desk at work or in your wallet. The more places you see it, the more you will be reminded to work towards your goals and dreams.

10. Review Daily

Take a moment to review your board each day – maybe in the morning and at night. Stop and fill your senses with your dreams and goals. Connect with your 'why' and the feelings of success you will experience once you have achieved your vision.

11. Acknowledge and Celebrate

Throughout the year, acknowledge and celebrate the goals you have achieved.

12. Progress and Revise

Each year, before creating your new board, go back and revise to see what has been achieved and the progress you have made.

My 2019 Vision Board

My Business Vision Board

Vision Board by Jaxon Dalton Steel, 10 years old.

MORE SUCCESS STRATEGIES

Visualisation

Jack Canfield, author of the *Chicken Soup of the Soul* series and known as America's #1 Success Coach, says, "Daily rituals help to establish the right balance between thinking about the future and living in the moment. Start by picking a time of during which you'll review your goals and visualise your success. Ideally, do this twice a day – first thing in the morning and right before you go to bed."

Visualisation activates the creative powers of the subconscious and helps the RAS focus on what you want, and notice things that may have escaped your attention. By visualising what you want, you will unexpectedly start to do things that move yourself closer to becoming the person you want to be and having the life you want to live. People will start to show up in your life, resources will appear, and opportunities needed to further your goals will materialise.

When you are visualising, imagine the colours, people, voices, what others will say, what you say to yourself, and allow yourself to feel the feelings achieving your success deeply. Make it as realistic as possible.

Practice a Grateful & Abundant Mindset...

In his book, *Give and Take*, Adam Grant writes about neuroscience which shows that giving actually activates the reward and meaning centres in our brains, which send us pleasure and purpose signals when we act for the benefit of others.

> *One study of more than 2,800 Americans over age twenty-four showed that volunteering predicted increases in happiness, life satisfaction, and self-esteem—and decreases in depression—a year later. And for adults over sixty-five, those who volunteered saw a drop in depression over an eight-year period.*

This got me thinking about giving and receiving and six lessons of gratitude and abundance I have learned...

Lesson 1: Leave a Little

Every week for the last 19 years my family has gone to the local vegetable market to get our weekly fresh vegetables. It has always been a family affair. The atmosphere at the market, in my opinion, is always made better when a guitarist or singer is there. Since the children have been small, I have always stopped, danced to the music with my children and left the performer our spare coins from our weekly shop. Leaving the small change in gratitude of their efforts is also about us knowing that there is always something left to give, no matter how tight the budget is that week. This is similar to a great friend who was taught to leave food on his plate, to teach his brain there is always enough – abundance.

Lesson 2: Want What You Have

We live in a society where people always seem to want more. We are bombarded with no interest on purchases, buy now and don't pay for 18 months and advertising everywhere you turn. It seems that people can never be satisfied as they always want more. I recently saw a poster that said "Want to be Rich? – Just want what you already have."

I love this on so many levels. When our children were younger, while cleaning out their rooms, they discovered so many toys, activities, books and treasures that they suddenly wanted! As I was ready to throw much of it out, the all too familiar words were uttered, "Oh, I want that!" Perhaps the key to diminishing our wants is to go through our belongings and see what we do have.

Gratitude turns what we have into enough.

- Melody Beattie

Lesson 3: Make Room

Years ago, I learned about the concept of a vacuum – not the appliance, but the physics definition; "A volume of space that is essentially empty of matter, void or vacant." Where there is a vacuum, void of space, it must be filled.

Translated, for this context, this means throwing out unwanted belongings to make room for the new. This has been popularised by Marie Kondo, organisation expert and best-selling author of, *The Life-Changing Magic of Tidying Up: The Japanese Art of Decluttering and Organising*.

Over the years I have found this to be true… I don't have a huge wardrobe of clothes (although my husband might disagree.) Every time I clean it out, I give my presenting clothes to Dress For Success, an organisation that helps women dress well for interviews to get back into the workforce. The rest of the clothes go to the second hand shop. The next week I always find the perfect outfit and it is nearly always discounted! You have to make the space, for it to be filled!

Lesson 4: Be Clear on Your Motivation

I recall crying on a colleague's shoulder once, because I felt very under appreciated and no-one had said thank you for the work I had done. My colleague asked, "Is that why you did it- for the acknowledgement?"

This took me aback and I had to reflect very hard on this. Yes, I love the acknowledgement, the thank-you's, the accolades... and was this truly why I did something? I thought some more and wondered. Would I still do it if I knew no-one was watching? If no-one knew it was me? This does not mean you should not give positive feedback, say thank you or give acknowledgement, as it is a human desire to be needed, wanted and loved. What I am suggesting is to simply look at the motivation behind your actions. Another of my favourite quotes is,

> *Integrity is doing the right thing, even when no one is watching.*
>
> — C.S. Lewis

Lesson 5: Give to Get

Understand the yin and yang of life. If you want respect you first need to give it. If you want love, first you must love yourself. If you want to be rich, share what you have. However, giving on its own is not enough, you must also be willing to receive. Grant Adams writes; "Since some givers tend to put others' interests ahead of their own, they often help others at the expense of their own well-being, placing themselves at risk for burnout." Practice being balanced and being able to graciously receive alongside your giving.

Lesson 6: Actively Practice Gratitude

The ability to find gratitude each day is something successful people have in common. Even on those challenging and dark days, there is always something to be grateful for. If you are new to this give it a go. At the end of each day, pause and recall or find three things you are grateful for that day. If you are unsure where to start, begin with your everyday basics, food, shelter, friends, family etc. If you have been practicing gratitude for a while, deepen your practice by searching beyond the surface and deeply feeling your gratefulness. Let it encapsulate your heart.

> *Grateful people are happy people. The more things you're grateful for, the happier you will be.*
>
> - Roy T. Bennett

Gratitude will give you a perspective on your life that will change you forever. In April 2018 I set up a private Facebook Group and invited others to share their daily three gratitudes. By the end of the month there were 40 people practicing daily gratitude. At the writing of this book, 18 months later, there are over 500 people on this page and the feedback has been astounding. One of our gratitudians recently wrote;

> *I am more positive and patient, have much less of a complaining culture and value people more.*

Another said;

> *Only after three short weeks of practicing gratitude I am so different. I'm better equipped to deal with the unpredictable, I now focus on what I can control and am less anxious and far more positive and productive.*

Another recently wrote after sharing her 9 month journey on the gratitude page;

> *My story is a real life example of how being grateful multiplies the positive results.*

Some Questions To Ponder

What are you (or could you) be grateful for in your life?
Who do you need to become to live the life of your dreams?
What do you need to 'let go of' in order to attract what you really want and deserve?
What do you do when no-one is watching?
How do you demonstrate abundance in your life?

> *When you are grateful, fear disappears, and abundance appears.*
>
> — Anthony Robbins

FINAL THOUGHTS

Creating the life of your dreams is a true privilege and one journey that most people do not take. It is hard, difficult and challenging at the best of times and super rewarding in the long run. It is not for the faint hearted – it takes courage, commitment and sacrifice.

It is a journey – and while that might sound like a cliché, it is the struggle that makes us strong.

One thing I have learned, as I have been designing my life for a couple of decades now, is that you never know what is around the corner and it is part of the exciting adventure.

Life is either a daring adventure – or nothing at all.
- Helen Keller

I have created a life where I am able to travel the world and have an impact on others and make deep connections with my loved ones and friends. Your dreams do not have to be as lofty as others – and might even be bigger! It is your life, your choice, your design. Take the time to listen to your heart, your source and be guided by your intuition not your ego.

Remember, nothing is set in concrete. You can pivot and change direction at any time.

Step by step… one day at a time… one goal… one strategy at a time…

> *Life is like riding a bicycle. To keep balance, you must keep moving.*
>
> - Albert Einstein

Keep moving in the direction of your dreams...

Finally, I Wish You Enough

I wish you enough rain to make you appreciate the sun
I wish you enough happiness to keep your spirit alive
I wish you enough sadness so that you appreciate the smallest joys in life
I wish you enough gain to satisfy your ambitions
I wish you enough loss to appreciate all that you possess
I wish you enough love so you know just how special you are
I wish you enough hurt to make love even sweeter
I wish you enough dreams to cause your imagination to soar
I wish you enough reality to keep your feet on the ground
I wish you enough success to make you proud
I wish you enough failure to keep you humble
I wish you enough independence to accomplish your goals
I wish you enough dependence on others to keep your goals from being selfish
I wish you enough "hellos" to get you through the final "good-bye"

- Source unknown

GRATITUDE & THANKS

I have really loved putting this process and book together for you. As always, it doesn't happen without support and focus.

Firstly, to my teachers, advisors and mentors over the past 25 years. Your wisdom has transferred and caused me to not only live the life of my dreams, it has also allowed me to share this journey for others to follow. Thanks.

I am grateful to my friends who jumped at the chance to come to my first vision board workshops at my kitchen table and the people who have participated in public and online courses. Each time I facilitate this workshop I get further distinctions and ideas to improve the process.

To Travis Bell, Lauren Parsons, Rowena McEvoy and Glenn Capelli for your kind permission to add a small piece of your wisdom into this book.

To Jessica Youmans for your editing work on the manuscript and my design team, Saravanan Ponnaiyan and Farhan Ahmad – you make my words look so beautiful on the page.

To the current and past team at Spectrum, thanks and gratitude for all the help, advice, feedback and new learning and insights. You are an awesome group of people, focused on our goal of being At The Heart of Teaching and Learning. Thanks for believing in my vision and keeping everything ticking while I wrote.

To my children, my rainbows and sunshine, Hamish & Sasha... you have shared this journey with me and allowed me to coach you to do the same. I'm enjoying watching you in your late teens, start to design your life and experience the richness life offers.

Finally, and best of all, to the man of my dreams, Denny. The shared experience is something so special and I am eternally grateful to have you by my side on our journey. Your support, coaching, prodding and always being there for me with open arms and those sparkly blue eyes is truly appreciated and valued.

BIBLIOGRAPHY

Boyes, Karen Tui; (2019) *Your Weekly Gratitude Focus.* Spectrum Education, NZ

Boyes, Karen Tui; (2019) *Project Genius – Big Learning for Young Geniuses.* Spectrum Education, NZ

Boyes, Karen Tui; (2018) *Study Smart – Your Essential Guide to Passing Tests and Exams.* Spectrum Education, NZ

Canfield, Jack; *How To Create an Empowering Vision Board.* www.jackcanfield.com

Capelli, Glenn; (2009) *Thinking Caps.* Capa, Australia

Clear, James; (2018) *Atomic Habits - An Easy & Proven Way to Build Good Habits & Break Bad Ones.* Penguin Random House.

Costa, Arthur & Kallick, Bena (2008) *Learning and Leading with Habits of Mind : 16 Essential Characteristics for Success.* ASCD, USA

Dweck, Carol. (2006) *Mindset: The New Psychology of Success.* Random House

Grant, Adam; (2014) *Give and Take- Why Helping Others Drives Our Success.* Penguin Books

Hardy, Benjamin; *How Planning to Fail Can Help You Succeed.* www.fastcompany.com

Klaus, Peggy; (2003) BRAG! *The Art of Tooting Your Horn Without Blowing It.* Warner Books, New York

Kwondo, Marie; (2016) The Life-Changing Magic of Tidying Up: The Japanese Art of Decluttering and Organizing CreateSpace Independent Publishing Platform

Manson, Mark (2018) *The Subtle Art of Not Giving a F*ck : A Counterintuitive Approach to Living a Good Life.* HarperCollins, USA

Parsons, Lauren; (2015) *The Quality of Your Thoughts Determines the Quality of Your Life.* www.laurenparsonswellbeing.com

Sharma, Robin (2018) *The 5 AM Club: Own Your Morning. Elevate Your Life.* HarperCollins, UK

Sugars, Brad; *Entrepreneur Business School.* Action International

Sinek, Simon; (2011) Start With Why: How Great Leaders Inspire Everyone To Take Action. Penguin

Sinek, Simon, et al; (2017) *Find Your Why- A Practical Guide for Discovering Purpose for You and Your Team.* Penguin

PROFESSIONAL DEVELOPMENT OPTIONS WITH KAREN

Award winning international educator Karen Tui Boyes is available to present to and work with Teachers, Students and Parents. Below are some options for you to be able to access Karen's expertise and knowledge to assist you in raising achievement and preparing students for the world ahead. All Professional Learning Development is personalised to the needs of your students, teachers & goals of the school/conference or organisation.

Ways you might engage Karen to work with Teachers, Students & Parents...

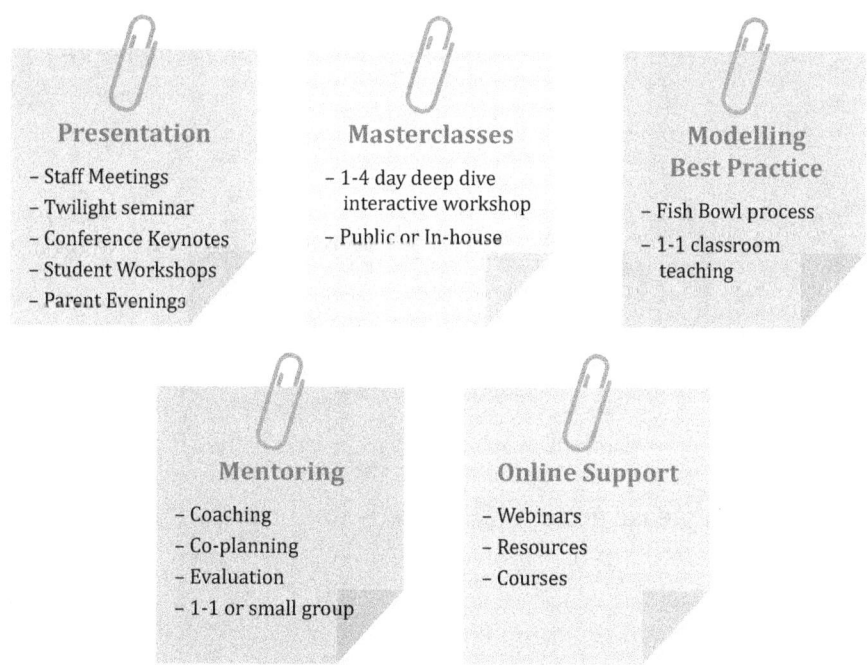

Presentation
- Staff Meetings
- Twilight seminar
- Conference Keynotes
- Student Workshops
- Parent Evenings

Masterclasses
- 1-4 day deep dive interactive workshop
- Public or In-house

Modelling Best Practice
- Fish Bowl process
- 1-1 classroom teaching

Mentoring
- Coaching
- Co-planning
- Evaluation
- 1-1 or small group

Online Support
- Webinars
- Resources
- Courses

Topics include:

For more information please go to: www.spectrumeducation.com/pld-kahui-ako

MORE BOOKS & PUBLICATIONS BY KAREN TUI BOYES

Find out more at www.spectrumeducation.com

www.ingramcontent.com/pod-product-compliance
Lightning Source LLC
Chambersburg PA
CBHW060426010526
44118CB00017B/2380